Halloween

MW01173866

October 31 was the New Year's Eve of the Celts who lived in Britain and northern Europe around 2,000 years ago. On that night they would gather with their priests, called Druids. They feasted and told stories of their ancestors. The Celts believed that the spirits of those who had died during the year were wandering around on that night, cold, lonely, hungry, and apt to play tricks, so the Celts left offerings of food and drink on their doorsteps. Those who had to go outside on that scary night carried lanterns and wore disguises so the spirits would not recognize them.

When church leaders were trying to convert the Celts in the early days of Christianity, they made November 1 and 2 All Saints' Day and All Souls' Day, both of which recognized the spirits of the dead. October 31 then became the Eve of All Saints' (or All Hallows) Day, which was eventually shortened to *Halloween*. Although the customs have been modified over the years, they remain basically the same— lanterns, gifts of food, and scary disguises.

Activities

- Discuss Halloween with the children. Explain that it is an enjoyable time, not a scary time.

- Talk about trick-or-treating. Have the class discuss street safety and reflective clothing. Remind children that all of the "treats" they receive need to be checked prior to eating.

- Have the students do some Halloween research. Assign the following questions to various individuals or groups of children. Upon completion, have all share their information.

   1. How did witches and black cats come to be associated with Halloween?
   2. Who was the original jack-o'-lantern and how did he get his name?
   3. Where did people first begin to trick or treat?
   4. Who brought this custom to the United States?
   5. In which modern country is Halloween a national holiday?

- Create tissue paper ghosts. Ball up one tissue and then take another and lay it out flat. Put the ball in the middle of the flat tissue. Fold over and tie a piece of yarn around the ball to form a head. Put eyes on with a black marker. Finally, hang the ghosts from the ceiling.

- Make sponge-paint orange pumpkins. Cut an old sponge into the shape of a pumpkin. Put orange tempera paint into a foam tray. Have the children stamp the design onto construction paper. They may add features of a jack-o'-lantern after the paint dries.

Bibliography

Balestrino, Phillip. *The Skeleton Inside You.* HarperCollins, 1989.

Brown, Ruth. *A Dark, Dark Tale.* Dial, 1981.

Cole, Joanna. *The Magic School Bus Inside the Human Body.* Scholastic, 1992.

Gross, Ruth Belov. *A Book About Your Skeleton.* Scholastic, 1994

Miller, Edna. *Mousekin's Golden House.* Simon and Schuster, 1990.

Drawing Halloween Characters

(Note: You may want to define "oval" shape for students prior to this drawing assignment.)

Directions: Draw a witch. Follow the steps in each box.

1. Draw an oval for the body.

2. Add an oval head. Put a skinny oval on top for a hat brim and add a triangle top.

3. Draw a set of connecting ovals for arms, legs, hands, and feet.

4. Add hair, a face, and a broom.

Draw your own witch here.

Drawing Halloween Characters *(cont.)*

Directions: Draw a cat. Follow the steps in each box.

1. Draw half an oval. 	4. Complete your cat with whiskers and hair to make your cat look scary. 
2. Draw another half oval inside the first oval. 	Draw your Halloween cat here.
3. Add eyebrows, eyes, nose, mouth, and ear shapes as shown. 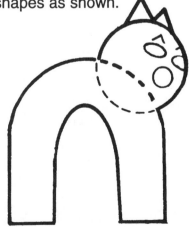	

Funnybones

Author: Janet and Allan Ahlberg

Publisher: Mulberry Books, 1980 (*available in Canada, Gage Distributors; U.K., Mammoth; AUS, Kirby Book Co.*)

Summary: This book tells of the adventure experienced by three skeletons (an adult, a child, and a dog) who go for a walk on a dark, dark night.

Related Holiday: Halloween is celebrated on October 31 in Great Britain, Ireland, Canada, and the United States as the evening before the feast of All Saints' Day.

Related Poetry: "Skeleton Parade" by Jack Prelutsky and "On Halloween" by Aileen Fisher, *Read-Aloud Rhymes for the Very Young* (Alfred A. Knopf, 1986); "Halloween" by Ivy O. Eastwick and "Look at That!" by Lilian Moore, *Side by Side: Poems to Read Together* (Simon & Schuster, 1988).

Related Songs: Traditional song "Dem Bones"

Connecting Activities:

- As you read this book to your children, call attention to the skeletons of different animals. Encourage your children to guess what these animals are.

- Discuss with your children why the authors named the book *Funnybones*. Have your students vote whether they like this title. What other titles do your students believe would be suitable?

- Discuss the idiom "tickled my funnybone" and question where one's funnybone is. Decide if there really is a funnybone in the human skeleton. Verify your decision in a reference book.

- Read several other books that follow the same "dark, dark" pattern, such as *A Dark, Dark Tale* by Ruth Brown and *In a Dark, Dark Wood* by June Melser and Joy Cowley. Compare and contrast the story elements such as location, setting, atmosphere created by the art work, and ending.

- Make writing innovations following the same "dark, dark" pattern. Children may write their own innovations, or you can guide them as a class by writing the sentences suggested by your students on sentence strips and placing them in a pocket chart for all to read.

- Have your children create their own skeletons, using white straws or foam packing peanuts. Children may make individual human skeletons on 12" x 18" (30 cm x 45 cm) pieces of black construction paper. These skeletons may be displayed on a long bulletin board or in the hallway along a tack strip. (You might copy the poem "Skeleton Parade" by Jack Prelutsky on a large sheet of chart paper to display with your students' skeletons to create your own parade of skeletons.)

- For a variation, encourage your students to make a mural of zoo animal skeletons similar to the ones found in the book, by using white chalk on a long piece of black butcher paper. Have children guess what animals their classmates created. Make labels to identify the animals, but hide the words under the flap to check their guess.

- Do a K-W-L (Know-Want to know-Learned) activity with your students. List on a chart the facts that they **know** about skeletons. Have them decide what they **want** to know about them. Invite a doctor, nurse, or any other qualified person to come into the classroom to explain the importance of the skeleton, as well as how the bones, joints, and muscles work together. Read factual books such as *A Book About Your Skeleton* by Ruth Belov Gross, *The Skeleton Inside You* by Phillip Balestrino, *What's Inside My Body?* by DK Direct Limited, and *The Magic School Bus Inside the Human Body* by Joanna Cole. Have your students list on the chart what they have **learned** about skeletons.

- Ask students to estimate how many bones there are in the human skeleton. Bring a model skeleton into your classroom and count the exact number of bones (206). Verify your count by checking in a reference book. Compare your estimate to the actual number.

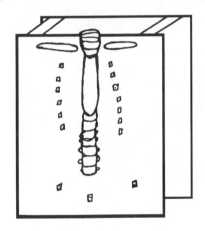

- Attach labels to the major bones on a life-size skeleton or on a cardboard skeleton posted in the room. You could make a "sandwich-board" learning center activity for the science area in your classroom. Use two sheets of 18" x 24" (46 cm x 61 cm) white tagboard (one for the front and one for the back). Use two strips of 3" x 8" (8 cm x 20 cm) white tagboard to attach the front and the back pieces together at the shoulders. Draw the outline of the body on the front and back with a marker. Cut bones out of the other scraps of tagboard. Laminate the "sandwich-board," the connecting strips, and the bones. Attach the bones to the correct places on the front and back of the body pieces with Velcro. Children remove and then replace the bones to the "sandwich-board" while one child wears it.

- Assess your students' understanding of the human skeleton by having them complete the human skeleton activity on the following page.

The Human Skeleton

Directions: Label the skeleton parts by writing the words from the box on the lines.

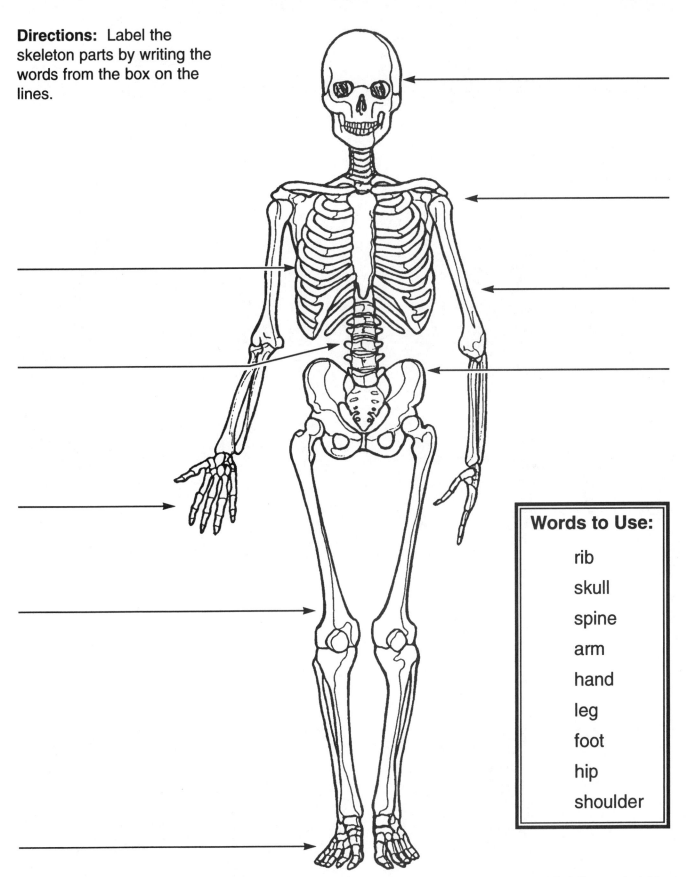

Words to Use:

rib

skull

spine

arm

hand

leg

foot

hip

shoulder

How Many Pumpkins?

Name _____

1. Count the pumpkins on the vine.
2. Write the number on the line.
3. Color the pumpkins and vine.

_____ _____

_____ _____

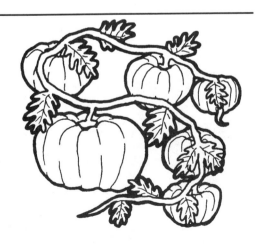

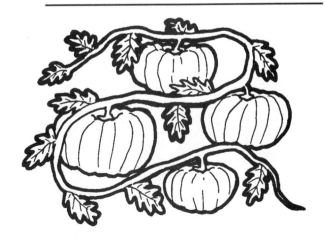

_____ _____

#787 Halloween Activities

Pumpkin Addition

Name _____   Date _____

Find the sums. Then write the word name of each answer on the lines. One has been done

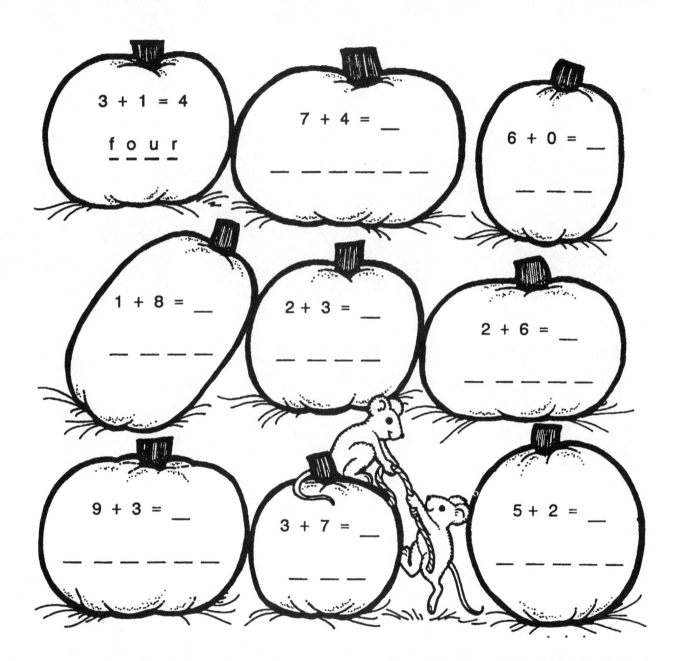

3 + 1 = 4

f o u r
_ _ _ _

7 + 4 = __

_ _ _ _ _

6 + 0 = __

_ _ _

1 + 8 = __

_ _ _ _

2 + 3 = __

_ _ _ _

2 + 6 = __

_ _ _ _ _

9 + 3 = __

_ _ _ _ _

3 + 7 = __

_ _ _

5 + 2 = __

_ _ _ _ _

Can't remember how to spell a number name? Use this word bank to help you.

seven	eight	nine
ten	six	twelve
five	eleven	four

Make Your Own Faces!

Name _____   Date_____

Draw a different face on each pumpkin. Write a title or name for each one.

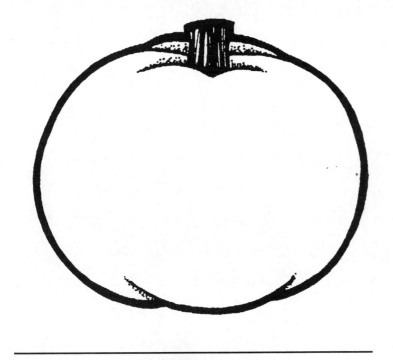

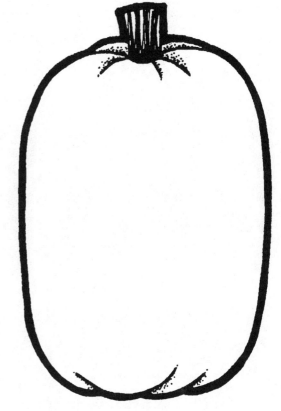

Halloween Story

(Halloween, October 31)

Name _____   Date _____

Read the paragraph below. Fill in the blanks with words from the Word Bank below

_____ 31 is a special _____ for children in

the United States and Canada. It is Halloween, a time when _____

dress up as monsters, _____, animals, or other characters. They go from

house to house to collect _____ and treats.

"_____!" is what they say. Sometimes

_____ are held in the evening. _____ is a popular beverage, and

bobbing for _____ is a _____ that everyone can

enjoy.

Trick or Treat	**children**	**parties**
game	**October**	**cider**
candy	**ghosts**	**holiday**
Halloween	**apples**	**candle**

Halloween Riddles

Out of the graveyard
Filled with stones,
No hair or skin,
I'm nothing but bones.
What am I?

My hat is black.
My face is green.
My laugh is mean.
I ride a broom
On Halloween.
What am I?

The shadows chase the sun away.
The stars come out to dance and play.
I'm at the end of another day.
What am I?

I fly at night.
I hunt by sound.
I live in a cave
And sleep upside down.
People are scared;
They shouldn't be.
I eat mice and bugs.
Please don't hurt me.
What am I?

I grew on a vine,
Right on the ground.
I have a big smile,
All orange and round.
What am I?

My eyes are gold.
My fur is black.
I hiss and spit
And arch my back.
My claws are sharp.
I might attack.
What am I?

My door is gone.
My windows cracked.
Ghosts float through walls
And then float back.
You hear strange noises,
Bam, bang, and whack.
What am I?

I like to stay
Just out of sight.
If you see me,
I might be white.
I float through houses
In the black of night.
What am I?

Halloween Weaving

Materials: black 12" x 18" (30 cm x 45 cm) construction paper, strips of various widths of orange construction paper cut into 12" (30 cm) lengths, scissors, glue, pencil

Directions: Have students follow the steps below to create their own weaving pattern.

1 Fold the black paper in half widthwise.	**2** Draw a parallel pencil line 1" (2.54 cm) from the open edges.
3 Cut curved, straight, or zigzag lines from the fold up to the 1" line. Open the paper.	**4** Weave strips of orange paper across the width of the black paper. Experiment leaving spaces, going under one, over two, etc.

When the design is complete, have students glue the ends of the strips down and trim off the extra.

Variations: Try weaving with any color paper, or use magazines, newspaper, or wallpaper cut in strips. Weave ribbon, yarn, or straw into the picture.

Witch's Mask and Three-D Ghost

Witch's Mask in Profile

Materials: large paper egg carton (18 egg size), black construction paper, yarn, stapler, scissors, tempera paint (varied colors)

Directions: Cut the top off a large egg carton. Paint this part green, brown, or any color you want the witch to be. Cut four egg cups off and paint them the same colors. Glue the cups in an "L" shape for a nose and staple to the carton top. Cut eye holes and paint an eyebrow above one eye hole. Paint hair around the other eye hole. Attach yarn over the top for more hair. Paint a smile or a cackling mouth and crooked teeth. Staple a black pointed hat to the top. Paint a black wart on the nose. Attach yarn to the edges as shown to wear the mask.

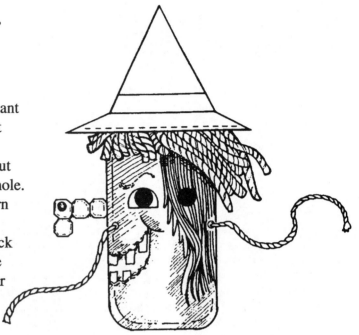

Three-D Ghost

Materials: 30" (70 cm) squares of cheesecloth (two per student), fabric stiffener (available at craft or fabric stores), white glue, scissors, margarine cups or other disposable bowls, plastic wrap (about two feet per student), eight oz. (236 mL) plastic or foam cups, paper tape, black felt, aluminum foil, plastic bags to cover work area

Directions: Roll a piece of aluminum foil into a two-inch (5 cm) ball shape. Tape it to the bottom of a paper or foam cup (this becomes the ghost figure). Place the figure upside down on the plastic bag and cover it with plastic wrap. Place one square of cheesecloth over the other for double thickness. Dip the cheesecloth (fold into quarters or eighths first) into a bowl of fabric stiffener and squeeze out excess. Unfold and drape cheesecloth over the plastic-wrapped figure. Crimp edges and shape to create desired effect. Let dry overnight. Lift from mold and glue felt eyes and mouth on. Add accessories.

Jack-O'-Lantern Wreath

Materials: cardboard doughnut shape about eight inches (20 cm) in diameter (or a paper plate with the center cut out), orange yarn, scissors, black construction paper scraps, tape

Directions: Have the children follow the steps below.

1. Wrap the yarn one time around the cardboard doughnut and secure the end with a knot.

2. Continue wrapping the yarn through the hole and around the cardboard to cover all the doughnut.

3. After the cardboard is completely covered, secure the loose end of the yarn by tying it to the wrapped yarn. Trim any excess.

4. Use the scraps of black construction paper to cut out two eyes, a nose, and a mouth.

5. Tape each facial feature to a single piece of yarn. Tie the loose ends of the yarn to the top of the doughnut so the features hang down in the hole of the doughnut shape.

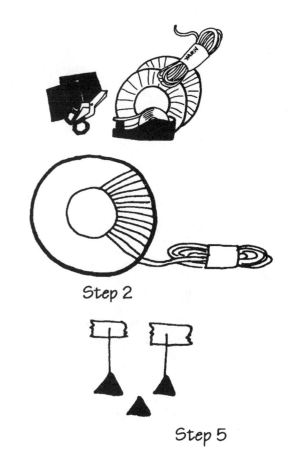

Step 2

Step 5

More Ideas

- To make wrapping the yarn through the hole of the doughnut shape easier, take one end from the skein and wrap it around a craft stick. Continue wrapping the stick until it is fat with yarn. The stick will go through the hole easier than an entire skein.

- Cut yarn in different fall colors and different lengths. Tie the ends together and wrap them around the wreath to give it a variegated yarn look. Use additional yarn or glue to attach real or imitation fall leaves.

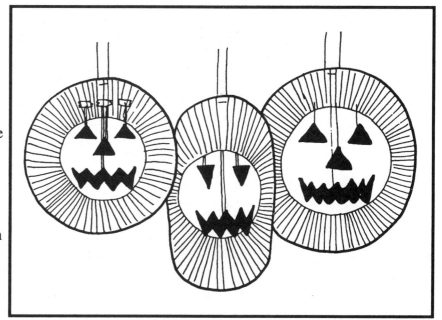

Create Your Own Monster

Directions: Draw a picture of a Halloween monster and color it. Then give it a name.

_____ by _____
Monster's Name   My Name

A Tricky Treat Bag

Materials: scissors, glue, crayons or markers, magazines, candy wrappers (optional), ribbon or yarn, hole punch and hole reinforcers or stapler, paper bag

Directions: Cut out pictures of candy and other treats and paste onto the front of the paper bag. (You may also use candy wrappers.) With crayons or markers, write the words "Trick or Treat" at the top of the bag. Staple ribbon or yarn to the top of each side of the paper bag for a handle or punch a hole on either side of the bag. Put a reinforcer around both sides of each hole. String yarn or ribbon through the holes.

- -

Pet Trick-or-Treat Bag

If your pet could go trick or treating, what would he/she collect? Draw or cut out pictures from books and magazines to put on the paper bag shape.

Don't have a pet? Make one up or adopt a dinosaur for a pet.